Spaces and Reflections

A journal for writing

Copyright © 2020 by Chaplain Sharon

All rights reserved. No part of this book may be reproduced or used in any manner without written permission of the copyright owner except for the use of quotations in a book review.

Quotations in this work derive from the thoughts and inspiration of the author and were not directly quoted from any outside sources.

Chaplain Life

www.chaplainlife.org
www.chaplaingear.com

Follow us on Social Media
Twitter/IG/Facebook @chaplaingear
Tag us with #chaplaingear #chaplainlife

Spaces and Reflections

There is individuality and autonomy in certain spaces. Space can be freedom, inspiration, vision. Space can be hope, new ideas, reflections of the present and across time. May these pages serve as a space of what you desire and need them to be just for you. This journal was created as a space of self-care and reflection for anyone who desires to write within its pages.

Peace and Light,
Chaplain Sharon

Generosity is a gift that may yield the unseen.

The gift of you is unique enough.

Think, live, and dream outside of the box.

Boxes are often too small anyway.

When days are difficult, may you be reminded of your inspirational source(s).

Replenishing the soul is like a refreshing wind that energizes one to lift the arms, tilt the head back, and bask in its refreshing benefits.

YOU DESERVE THE GIFT OF SELF-CARE.

**Love is healing.
Absorb its rays.**
♥

One of the most beautiful things to wear can simply be a smile. ☺

*Intuition.
Trust it.*

Bring to the world, your best and authentic self.

Stillness can also speak.

> **Emotions are like keys, unlocking a world of information about ourselves and others. Access them.**

Achieving greater balance is often individual and unique.

Opportunities may come at times to broaden our horizons.

DREAMS AND VISIONS ARE WORTHY OF OUR ATTENTION.

LAUGH.

                  SMILE.

                                    REJOICE.

Some say that tears cleanse. Maybe they have special healing powers too.

> **To be human is to not have all the answers.**

Thank You.

Thank you

www.ingramcontent.com/pod-product-compliance
Lightning Source LLC
Chambersburg PA
CBHW071404080526
44587CB00017B/3174